CLOSE THE DOOR

What Happens In the Closet Stays in the Closet!

Not Everyone Is Mature Enough to be Present to Watch You Press Through
Your Proclivities in Prayer

TAMMY M. ISAAC, MDiv

DEDICATION

This book is dedicated to my beloved mother Theresa Isaac Lewis who has gone on to be with God in heaven.
I love and miss her so much. My mother was a part of several prayer ministry phone lines. One day while flipping through her bible a piece of paper fell out. It was the phone list of the prayer lines she had participated in. I remember whenever we traveled together she would never miss her prayer lines no matter where we were or what time it was. Once while on a trip to Kentucky I woke up to find my mother in the hotel closet on one of her prayer lines. She understood the concept and took it literally to go in the closet, close the door, and pray.

Below is a copy of the paper that fell out of her bible with the list of the prayer lines she was a part of. I am not sure if these prayer lines still exist today.

PRAYER-LINE

Time	Number	Name
5:00 am	712-432-0926 # 250-608	R. Johnson
5:30 am Satur-7:00am	605-475-4000 # 237-058	Diane Alk
6:00 am	712-432 0075 # 969 932	
8:00 am	712-775-7300 # 501-364	Bettey Linda
7:00 pm	605-477-2100 # 811-601	Catty
10:00 pm	559-546-1000 # 987-894	L. Brown
8:00 am	712-432-1601 #241-953	

James 5:14
Is any sick among you?
Let him call for the elders of the church, and let them pray over him anointing him with oil in the name of the LORD.

Mt. Zion M B church Prayer
713-631-2595

ACKNOWLEDGMENTS

I thank God for His love and unfailing compassion towards me. I am grateful for my siblings Heather, Frank, Jemma, and Timmy, who are my support system and the very essence of who my mom was. Many thanks to my dear friend Likeythia Blackmon who supports me in ministry. I would like to thank Bishop Roderick Johnson of New Beginning Church Supernatural in Houston, TX for always believing and seeing greatness in me. It was under his leadership that I was birthed into ministry and I learned what it meant and looked like to have a relationship with God in prayer and not just in the pulpit on Sunday mornings.

TABLE OF CONTENTS

*A*nd when thou prayest, thou shalt not be as the hypocrites are: for they love to pray standing in the synagogues and in the corners of the streets, that they may be seen of men. Verily I say unto you, they have their reward. But thou, when thou prayest, enter into thy closet, and when thou hast shut thy door, pray to thy Father which is in secret; and thy Father which seeth in secret shall reward thee openly. But when ye pray, use not vain repetitions, as the heathen do: for they think that they shall be heard for their much speaking. Be not ye therefore like unto them: for your Father knoweth what things ye have need of, before ye ask him. After this manner therefore pray ye: Our Father which art in heaven, Hallowed be thy name. Thy kingdom come, Thy will be done in earth, as it is in heaven. Give us this day our daily bread. And forgive us our debts, as we forgive our debtors. And lead us not into temptation, but deliver us from evil: For thine is the kingdom, and the power, and the glory, for ever. Amen.

—Matthew 6:5-13 (KJV)

This book began as a sermon, my very first sermon to be exact. On February 4, 2007, I preached from Matthew 6:5-13 on the topic "The Lord's Way to Pray". Since then it has evolved into what you are about to experience as Close the Door.

INTRODUCTION

The prayer-filled life "can show us the way into intimacy with God"… it is "the human longing for the practice of the presence of God", where we place all of our attention on God, "because through it we experience the divine rest that overcomes our alienation"[1], which is the foundation for a lifestyle of holiness, according to Foster, in his book "Streams of Living Water". We as Christians must learn to have a prayer life. We keep God in our circumstances and situation by living a lifestyle of prayer. When we go to God in prayer we remind ourselves just how much we need and depend on Him in our Christian spirituality. Spending time with God in prayer allows us as believers to develop an intimate relationship with the Father, which equips us to meet life's challenges and struggles. Prayer also allows us to grow spiritually, becoming more and more like Christ.

Without the act of prayer we would never be able to make it through the many dimensions of life that we face, especially through the dimensions of problems and situations that comes from temptations,

---

1   Richard J. Foster, *Streams of Living Water: Celebrating the Great Traditions of Christian Faith* (San Francisco: Harper San Francisco, 1998), 5.

trials of our faith, and afflictions. Many of us tend to find prayer challenging because prayer invites us to examine our conscience with regard to all the problems that afflict our lives. At the same time prayer is a way of confronting our life's challenges.

In today's Christian organizations there is no shortage of praying going on. There are prayer services, prayer lines, prayer groups, prayer meetings, prayer breakfasts, prayer conferences, etc. There is so much praying going on but yet so little of answered prayer. I believe a significant reason for this is because many of us don't understand how prayer works, thus making our prayers ineffective.

We read scriptures in the bible like *"Ask, and it will be given to you; seek, and you will find; knock, and it will be opened to you" Matthew 7:7*, and *"Whatever you ask in prayer, believe that you have received it, and it will be yours" Mark 11:24*. With these scriptures we make a b-line into prayer asking for the things we want and need without the knowledge of how to pray the scriptures effectively. We forget that it is the *"effectual fervent prayers that availeth much"*, (James 5:16). This leads to unanswered prayer leaving us with the question of why God isn't responding to our prayers. Perhaps God is not the blame.

Maybe, just maybe, we could be the blame. No, it's not because of something we did or that God doesn't love us or want the best for us. It could be that we simply need to be taught how to pray again. Over the course of my years growing in Christian ministry, I must be honest, I've had to learn to pray over and over again. Each time I came into new revelation and understanding of God and His word, I grew spiritually and my prayer life changed to be more effective with my growth. I know many of us pride ourselves on the ability to pray but if we are honest with ourselves there comes a time when just like Jesus' disciples, we need to ask, *"Lord, teach us how to pray" (Luke 11:1).* As Jesus lived among His disciples here on earth, the disciples experienced Jesus' prayer life. No doubt they saw a hundred percent of His prayers answered, and wanted to know how to have their prayers answered a hundred percent of the time as well, so they asked, "Lord, teach us to pray".

Prayer was and is an important part of the teachings of Jesus then and now. Those who Jesus taught to pray weren't people who didn't pray and have an established prayer life. Of course they had been praying for many years of their lives, it was their practice to be found praying. Their Jewish tradition required them to be disciplined in the practice of prayer from early childhood. At the beginning and ending of each day, for as long as they could remember, they had quoted the Shema, the Jewish confession of faith taken from Deuteronomy 6:4-5, along with other prayers and benedictions.

Praying three times a day at particular hours of the day as well as before and after every meal. In fact, some historians say that the average Jew, during the time of Jesus, prayed three to four hours a day, but The Lord's Prayer was a different way of praying from the common prayers of the Old Testament. Even with their customary practice of prayer there was something missing. It was sincerity. Praying with sincerity. Praying with sincerity means that one doesn't pray to be praised by people. Praying with sincerity means that we do not pray simply out of habit but rather pray from the heart. To pray sincerely is to pray beyond memorized prayers repeated over and over, such as we do with The Lord's Prayer.

The Lord's Prayer is not a set form that Jesus himself prayed or asked His disciples to pray, but it illustrates the type of prayer that provides a pattern for properly ordering the priorities of the kingdom; first God, then human needs. In Matthew chapter 6, Jesus takes the disciples through the different ways many individuals have prayed in the past, and then He draws them into a new type of prayer that is designed to cover them through various seasons of their lives. By covering various aspects of the character of God, and areas of personal supplication, Christians to this day have a pattern by which we can come before God in prayer.

Praying The Lord's Prayer became a different approach to God than the Jews were used to, but an effective way nonetheless to pray for answered prayer. Then and now the caution is not to get caught up in the ritualized nature of The Lord's Prayer, but rather to embrace the teaching of The Lord's Prayer and to pray in a God centered manner, as opposed to a self-centered way. As we enter into our prayer closets and close the door, in a time of communion and "holy concealment"[2] with God, putting our petitions before Him, and pouring out our hearts and souls and our needs, we will see the manifestation of answered prayers.

---

2   John J. Parsons, "The Secret Place of the Most High: Dwelling in the Shadow of Shaddi," Hebrew for Christians, accessed February 20, 2019, https:/www.hebrew4christians.com/Meditations/Secret/secret.html.

Praying for many of us has its foundation in our childhood.

1

Where it all Began

For as long as I can remember, I have always attended church. My mother was very active in our church and even worked fulltime for our church for more than 14 years, so I practically grew up in the church. However, it wasn't until around the age of 23 that I really began to establish a right relationship with God. It was then that I rededicated my life unto the Lord and sought to develop a life-style of daily prayer.

However, I struggled to form a habit of praying. I found it to be quiet difficult. I really didn't understand how prayer was to work in my life by talking openly and not actually having someone present to make gestures to as I spoke as a sign of receiving and understanding what I was saying, or even to embrace and join in on the emotions that I shared. You know, it's kind of like having your best friend sitting with you listening to the highs and lows of your day, about a new relationship you are in, the weight you have gained, the sadness you feel, the joy of a new job or promotion, etc. Your best friend will engage you and share in your various emotions as you load them down with all of your life experiences. In fact, what I experienced when I began to pray was the exact opposite of what it would be like if I was actually talking to my best friend.

Charles and Myrtle Fillmore, a Kansas City, Missouri, couple, started a prayer movement back in the 1800's. Myrtle was quoted in a blog entitled: *The Importance of Prayer and Meditation*; she stated that prayers are not "sent" anywhere, she said "prayer is an exercise to change our thought habits and our living habits that we may set up a new and better activity, in accord with the divine law rather than with the suggestions we have received from various sources."[1]

Instead of feeling like I needed someone in front of me to talk to, I would soon learn that God didn't need to be in front of me, I had Him inside of me. My prayers weren't about me being heard, they were more about having a conscious encounter with God in my mind, body, and spirit. Conscious communion with God would change my perspective; giving me

---

1 Rosemary Ellen Guiley, "The Importance of Prayer and Meditation," Unity: A Positive Path for Spiritual Living, accessed May 21, 2019, http://www.unity.org/resources/articles/importance-prayer-and-meditation.

a new outlook on my situations and wisdom on how to face them.

As I was in the process of establishing a right relationship with God, it was a very difficult time in my life. I was separated from my husband who was one of my best friends that I would tell everything to but now I could no longer talk to him. Then there was my longtime best girlfriend whom it seemed very difficult to talk to about the things I was experiencing in this new walk with God because at the time she was not heading in the same direction spiritually as I was. I remember speaking with one of the Mothers of the Church I was attending at the time and she said to me "Baby, when you pray, talk to God like you are talking to your best friend. Just open your mouth and start talking to Him."

So, I remember one morning driving in to work, feeling very frustrated and bound in my situation of being separated from my husband; living back at home with my mother; laid off from my job; and now I was working a temporary job, and dealing with the stress of the lack of finances. I was trying to live this new life with God and leave my old life behind. Yet still trying to hold to who I was. As I was driving, I opened my mouth and started talking to God like I was talking to my best friend. I begin to tell him how my days have been, how things were going for me, and how I felt that morning along with thanks and appreciation for His daily grace and mercy. It definitely felt awkward and weird but I did it anyway.

After some days went by it still didn't feel normal, but I kept doing it because I knew that I needed to have this outlet and if I wasn't able to get it out I didn't know what would happen. I realized too that a lot of times when we talk to people we are not necessarily looking for people to respond or tell us how to fix things, or give us an answer to what we are going through. We literally just need to get it out of our system, sharing it with someone we trust and who is listening to us as if we matter and they care about what is happening with us. Saying our life experiences out loud to someone helps us to make sense of what is going on inside of our heads. As we speak and get things off our chest we release anxiety and feelings of being overwhelmed. Doing so will feel like a weight being lifted off our chest that's blocking our ability to breathe deeply, inhaling and exhaling. Our muscles then begin to relax and we begin to feel good, which allows us to mentally feel good. This is really a part of what prayer is.

God is listening. The bible tells us that even before we open our mouths to pray God has already heard us. This is an awesome thing. During my talks with God in the car I believed that God wasn't only hearing me, but He was sharing in my emotions, no matter how awkward it felt at the time.

What I began to understand is that prayer is nothing more and nothing less than holy (sacred) communion or communication with our God. Prayer is, us talking while God listens, and God talking while we listen. Prayer is beneficial in the life of every believer. For us it is a place of release, a place of rest, and a place where we receive from God. It is where we can pour out our entire self-unto God and become naked before him and not get talked about. "Prayer accomplishes many things. It develops our character to its highest state. It builds a mind that is always open to Spirit. Through prayer, we attain an interpenetrating consciousness with God's perfect life and love and power. We attain an oneness with God, thus achieving the example set by Jesus when he proclaimed, "I and the Father are one."[2]

Prayer has the potential and the power to change people, places, and possessions when done effectively. Yet, many Christians, like I once did; tend to feel insecure about their prayer life because we are not always sure that we are doing it right. "Prayer also enables us to become infused with divinely inspired ideas, which exalt our minds and our entire beings. Every divine idea you meditate upon and incorporate

---

2   Rosemary Ellen Guiley, "The Importance of Prayer and Meditation," Unity: A Positive Path for Spiritual Living, accessed May 21, 2019, http://www.unity.org/resources/articles/importance-prayer-and-meditation.

into your consciousness does a mighty regenerating, transforming, spiritualizing work in your mind, soul, [and] body and even in your outer world of affairs,"[3] Myrtle said.

Praying for many of us has its foundation in our childhood years when we learned to pray over our food: Grace

> *"God is great and God is good,*
> *And we thank him for our food;*
> *By his hand we must be fed,*
> *Give us Lord, our daily bread."*[4]

At night: Bed Time Prayer

> *"Now I lay me down to sleep.*
> *I pray the Lord my soul to keep.*
> *If I should die before I wake,*
> *I pray to God my soul to take."*[5]

---

3   Rosemary Ellen Guiley, "The Importance of Prayer and Meditation," Unity: A Positive Path for Spiritual Living, accessed May 21, 2019, http://www unity.org/resources/articles/importance-prayer-and-meditation.

4   Anonymous, *God Is Good and God Is Great Prayer*

5   David Barton, *New England Primer*, 7th ed. (Aledo, TX: WallBuilder Press, 1991).

And the prayer we learned to pray daily: The Lord's Prayer (Matthew 6:9-13)

"Our Father in heaven,
hallowed be your name,
your kingdom come,
your will be done,
on earth as it is in heaven.
Give us today our daily bread.
And forgive us our debts,
as we also have forgiven our debtors.
And lead us not into temptation,
but deliver us from the evil one."

The Lord's Prayer among Christian households was the first prayer that most children learned to pray growing up. In fact, as children, we could be found reciting The Lord's Prayer weekly during Sunday School class or Children's Church just like we could be found in our classrooms or at home reciting our ABC's and 123's.

Many people can't remember exactly when they learned their ABC's and 123's. They just know that one day they knew them. At some point a parent, guardian, family member, teacher, or baby sitter took the time to teach these fundamentals. It is for this very reason that right now today, they can sing the ABC song and recite their 123's with it rolling right off their tongue, without having to think about it. The same is with The Lord's Prayer for those who were raised in a Christian household. You might not be able to recall the exact day you learned The Lord's Prayer, you just know that you know it, and when it comes to reciting it, just like the ABC's and 123's, it just rolls right off your tongue without one thought of what you are saying. Because of this, just like the Jewish people Jesus references in Matthew 5:6 , believers tend to recite verbatim The Lord's Prayer out of ritual (because it's what Christians pray), out of reward (for the acceptance, applause, or approval of other believers), and out of requirement (because Jesus said believers should pray this way).

By doing so we miss out on the real purpose, power, and profit of praying in accordance to The Lord's Prayer. Instead of seeing prayer as an opportunity to ask God for something, it should be seen as a way of establishing an intimate relationship with God. When we pray we open our hearts, our souls, and our spirits to an intimate conversation with God. We invite Him to a time of intimate conversation, which is an expression of our faith and desire for relationship with God. As we develop our relationship with God in prayer it is the starting point for effective prayer that will release power to change people, places, and possessions.

Memorizing scripture has to go beyond ritual, requirement, and reward.

2

Going Beyond Memorization

Just like one day I woke up and realized that I knew my ABC's, 123's, and The Lord's Prayer, one day I woke up and realized I could no longer recite verbatim The Lord's Prayer. I had to pause and think about the words I was actually saying. This sounds bad for someone who is a Christian, a pastor, and a leader in the church. I was actually embarrassed within myself. In the middle of me teaching a bible study I began to recite The Lord's Prayer and in midstream I realized that I had forgotten the latter part of the verse. Unknowingly to my class I simply played it off by redirecting what I was initially going to say.

Once I got home I was bewildered at the fact I'd actually forgotten a scripture that I grew up reciting as a child. I wondered if it was a fluke, so I started to recite it out loud to myself and I still could not finish the entire passage. Surprisingly, I somehow had forgotten some parts of the prayer. I just couldn't figure it out.

This was the prayer that I grew up reciting, how could I have forgotten it? How could I have forgotten The Lord's Prayer? It's the staple prayer in every Christian household.

Going through the process of trying to figure out just how this happened, I realized that when I was growing up, in order to learn and remember The Lord's Prayer, those who taught me kept it before me every day as a foundational scripture to pray by. It was a part of my daily life helping to navigate my prayer life. I attended private school for many of my grade school years and I remember having to read and repeat, out loud, The Lord's Prayer each day; it was a part of our daily routine. There was not a day that we didn't recite The Lord's Prayer. Then, as I got older and no longer needed to read or be reminded of the words to The Lord's Prayer, I started quoting it, and eventually I was reciting it verbatim without pause; it just rolled off my tongue without me even having to think about it.

At this point the prayer had no meaning to me. It had now become something I did out of ritual; because it's what we prayed every day in private school, out of reward; for the acceptance, applause, or approval of my teachers or parents, and out of requirement; it was what we were told we had to pray. At that time, praying The Lord's Prayer had become more of a habit without any connection to God. I realized that I had forgotten the words to The Lord's Prayer because they were no longer a part of my daily prayer life; no longer the foundation of my prayers; and no longer navigating me through life. This saddened me, so I vowed to incorporate Matthew 6:9-13, The Lord's Prayer, as part of my daily scripture reading in an effort to commit it to memory and use it as a foundation for my prayer life once again.

Remembering scripture is an important aspect of our Christian walk. In God's word we are encouraged to "hide His word in our hearts" Psalm 119:11. God calls for His people to use His word as symbols in our hands, on our foreheads, and even to place them on our doorframes" Deuteronomy 6. "Committing things to memory allows us to choose words and images that shape our mind and heart. It gives the mind somewhere to go when all the media is turned off. It allows us to access divinely inspired thought and wisdom. And it works in us even when we are not conscious of its doing so."[1] Though I vowed to commit Matthew 6:9-13, The Lord's Prayer, to memory, I understood that just committing the scripture to memory was not good enough because I once "knew" the verses in the scripture but no longer had a connection to the meaning of its words or to

---

1   Adele Ahlberg Calhoun, *Spiritual Disciplines Handbook: Practices That Transform Us,* revised and expanded ed. (Downers Grove, Illinois: IVP Books, an imprint of InterVarsity Press, 2015), 195.

God. If we memorize The Lord's Prayer, we have in our possession the key to effective prayer that avails much (which means your prayers are full of power). But we must remember that when we only memorize The Lord's Prayer we only possess the key to effective prayer. God's power is always available to us, but if we do not use the key of prayer we cannot obtain His power in our lives for answered prayer. When I am given a key to a car I must use the key if I want to drive the car, but most importantly I have to use it first to unlock the car to get inside. The key is no good to use if we never use it to unlock the car. If the car key doesn't connect with the ignition, the power of the engine will not be ignited and I will never go anywhere.

With "the printing press, the increasing accessibility of books, the flood of information, the World Wide Web – all these make memorization less important"[2] and challenging at times. Therefore I drew on the spiritual discipline of memorization and meditation based on Adele Ahlberg Calhoun book, *Spiritual Disciplines Handbook "Practice That Transform Us"*. Calhoun says that "No doubt the ability to read and access to books and computers are wonderful gifts. But a mind so overwhelmed with information that nothing is known by the heart can leave the soul

---

2   Adele Ahlberg Calhoun, *Spiritual Disciplines Handbook: Practices That Transform Us*, revised and expanded ed. (Downers Grove, Illinois: IVP Books, an imprint of InterVarsity Press, 2015), 195.

at the mercy of the last mental image that tool our fancy."[3] I needed the scripture not just in my head but most importantly in my heart. What does this mean? This means that I need to know scripture well enough to be able to apply it to various life situations that I would have to face. I need to be able to quote it, believe it, and apply it. I need to have the ability to take what I've memorized and use it to help me navigate through life. If I can't apply it to my life and/or never think to do so, I might as well be memorizing something else other than scripture.

Effective prayer comes from relationship with the Father. In order to pray The Lord's way, you must first get to know Him and His ways through His word. We have been praying, but only out of what we have learned to memorize. Some of us have not recognized that our prayer lives have been powerless and unable to effect and change our surroundings. It is because we are relying on what we memorized as a babe in Christ. Memorizing scripture has to go beyond ritual, requirement, and reward.

---

3   Adele Ahlberg Calhoun, *Spiritual Disciplines Handbook: Practices That Transform Us*, revised and expanded ed. (Downers Grove, Illinois: IVP Books, an imprint of InterVarsity Press, 2015), 195.

Hypocrisy is the art of affecting qualities for
the purpose of pretending to an undeserved
virtue.
~ Benjamin F. Martin

3

The Great Pretender

In chapter 6 of the Gospel of Matthew, we find Jesus addressing the disciples on how they practiced their rituals that were required of them and how reward should not be their goal. He is in the middle of what seems like a preaching marathon known as The Sermon On The Mount when He introduces the subject of prayer, saying, *"And when thou prayest, thou shalt not be as the hypocrites are: for they love to pray standing in the synagogues and in the corners of the streets, that they may be seen of men. Verily I say unto you, they have their reward"*.

Jews prayed ritually three times a day; morning, afternoon, and night. During these times of prayer Jews would recite "the 19 blessings that make up the silent prayer, known in Hebrew as the Amidah."[1] They

---

1   Dov Bloom, "What Us the Amidah? The Silent Prayer," Chabad, accessed April 27, 2019, https://www.chabad.org/library/article_cdo/aid/3834226 /jewish/What-Is-the-Amidah-The-Silent-Prayer.htm.

all prayed the same prayer at the same time daily, and while the words of the prayer and timing of their prayer was important, it was even more important that they didn't lose sight of the fact that the most essential part of their prayers was the part that the heart plays in prayer. Charles G. Finney once said, "I am convinced that nothing in the whole Christian religion is so rarely attained as a praying heart." A person with a praying heart is a person who prays with their gaze upon the Lord. One who is concerned with the things that concerns God; one who has a heart connected to God, allowing the Word of God to sink deeply into their heart and allowing it to stay there until it consumes their total mind, body, and spirit, and eventually flowing out in their prayers and into their daily walk.

Praying three times a day meant that wherever they were at the scheduled times of prayer they would pray right where they were. Many of them were known to stand and pray on street corners in public (v5) where all could see and hear them as they prayed. Now, praying in public wasn't necessarily a bad thing. You can find several examples of public prayer in Scripture (I Kings 8:22-53; Ezra 9:6-15; Nehemiah 9:5-38; John 17:1-26). You can find numerous Christians throughout scripture, including Jesus, praying publicly. The issues with praying in public was a matter of right motives.

When praying in public with other people around, there tends to be the temptation to show-off, repeating all the "churchy" phrases you've heard others pray before. However, prayer was and can still be done in public and can also be done in private. *"My house will be called a house of prayer for all nations"*, (Isaiah 56:7). One of the purposes for the sanctuary is to be a place where believers meet for corporate prayer. It plays an important part in the life of the church among believers.

When Christians pray together in public it is called corporate prayer. Michael Lazio, Senior Pastor of Bethel House of Prayer Church, says that "The Church is a House of Prayer. As we assemble together we are the corporate expression of prayer."[2] Corporate prayer should be genuine, real, and from the heart. Corporate prayer unifies us as a body of believers. "As we regularly come together, we're reminded to maintain the unity of the Spirit in the bond of peace, Ephesians 4:3."[3] The most powerful form of prayer available to the body of Christ is united prayer. In addition, "Just as Jesus taught the disciples to pray (Matthew 6:10), when young believers listen to the prayers of the mature and faithful, their faith grows. Corporate prayer moves us beyond simplistic

2   Michael Lazio, "What Is a House of Prayer?," Bethel house of Prayer, accessed April 27, 2019, https://bethelhouseofprayer.com/about/what-is-a-house-of-prayer/.
3   Jennifer Oshman, "Six Reason the Church Needs Corporate Prayer," Unlocking The Bible, May 7, 2018, https://unlockingthebible.org/2018/05 six-reasons-the-church-needs-corporate-prayer/.

requests for ease or health or blessing (though those are worthy requests too) and teaches us to ask instead that we might be conformed to the likeness of Jesus (Romans 8:29)."[4] I am reminded of the time when I was struggling to find it comfortable to pray out loud in front of other people. It was a Tuesday night and I had arrived to bible study at the church I was attending at the time rather early, only to find that prayer meeting (corporate prayer) was going on. As I sat in on the prayer meeting I could hear the hearts of the older saints praying and crying out to God. Being moved to compassion within my heart I was compelled to pray out loud and cry out to God. I had been caught up in the divine conversation that was going on. I found myself joining the divine conversation as my heart lead me to pray out loud the matters of God and His concern for His people.

Corporate prayer also allows us to encourage and support other believers. When we come together as a group to pray, we must remember that God is present. We should think of our prayer time together as a divine conversation amongst our group members and God. Our prayers are to be God-focused, not an attempt to convince people of our righteousness. After all, even public prayers are for the primary purpose of speaking to God, not people.

---

4   Jennifer Oshman, "Six Reason the Church Needs Corporate Prayer," Unlocking The Bible, May 7, 2018, https://unlockingthebible.org/2018/05/six-reasons-the-church-needs-corporate-prayer/.

While the Church is a House of Prayer, we likewise are individually "a House of Prayer. *After you receive Jesus Christ as Savior, you become the temple of the Holy Spirit, I Corinthians 6:19."*[5] Therefore, corporate prayer is powerful, but so is prayer when done alone. Prayer can be done alone or with a group of people. "If the attitude is humble, focused on God's will and His plan for us, He will hear and respond. More importantly, we will be drawing closer to Him and taking on aspects of His character that are so essential to Christian life and the Kingdom of God."[6] However, there were some who loved to have people watch them pray in public in an effort to be seen as one who was religious and devout. You see, religious people tend to be people who do the right things, for the wrong reasons.

"Jesus called these men hypocrites for praying not to God but to an audience of people who [respected] them for their holiness."[7] In the Greek the word hypocrite is "hypokrites, hoop-ok-ree-tace'; an actor

5   Michael Lazio, "What Is a House of Prayer?," Bethel house of Prayer, accessed April 27, 2019, https://bethelhouseofprayer.com/about/what-is-a house-of-prayer/.

6   Richard T. Ritenbaugh, "Topical Studies: Bible Verses about Hypocritical Prayers," Bible Tools, accessed April 19, 2019, https://www.bibletools.org/index.cfm/fuseaction/Topical.show/RTD/cgg/ID/18091/Hypocritical-Prayers.htm.

7   Bruce B. Barton, *Matthew*, Life Application Bible Commentary (Wheaton, Ill.: Tyndale House Publishers, 1996), 112.

under an assumed character."[8] Hypocrites are actors who while on stage with the attention of an audience wore mask to hide their true identity. They performed acts of impersonation and deception. They also had to choose their words, the right sentiment, and the right gestures to receive the acceptance, approval, and acknowledgement of their audience.

When certain Jews prayed on the street corners, many of them where like actors who were simply acting out a script to perform for an audience that would give their approval (their reward), not God's. They were pretenders. Great. Pretenders. You know the people of which I am talking about. You know the ones in your church that only want to pray when they are on the microphone or down at the altar praying for people during the time of worship when they can be seen by the pastor and the congregants. Those who want to be heard praying by those who will affirm them and give them a pat on the back saying "You really prayed today", "you really mad the devil mad with that prayer", or "you brought down the house the way you prayed". These are the same people who you will never see in prayer meetings, at devotional prayer before worship service, or found participating in consecration without being accepted, approved, or

---

8   "G5273 - hypokritēs - Strong's Greek Lexicon (KJV)." Blue Letter Bible. Accessed 1 May, 2019. https://www.blueletterbible.org//lang/lexicon/lexicon. cfm?Strongs=G5273&t=KJV

acknowledged. These people are Pretenders. Great Pretenders, having the form of one who has a prayer life beyond corporate encounters of prayer.

The group called The Platters released a single titled "The Great Pretender" in 1955 that I believe best describes what we are when we pray as hypocrites. The lyrics to that song are as follows:

Oh yes I'm the great pretender (ooh ooh)
Pretending I'm doing well (ooh ooh)
My need is such I pretend too much
I'm lonely but no one can tell

Oh yes I'm the great pretender (ooh ooh)
Adrift in a world of my own (ooh ooh)
I play the game but to my real shame
You've left me to dream all alone

Too real is this feeling of make believe
Too real when I feel what my heart can't conceal

Ooh ooh yes I'm the great pretender (ooh ooh)
Just laughing and gay like a clown (ooh ooh)
I seem to be what I'm not (you see)
I'm wearing my heart like a crown
Pretending that you're still around[9]

---

9   Buck Ram, *The Great Pretender* (Berkeley, CA: Peermusic Publishing, 1955).

In the song, the lead singer, Tony Williams, describes himself as a hypocrite pretending to not be heartbroken as he deals with a relationship that has ended by denying it. That is why he labels himself as, "The Great Pretender". He is so caught up in his pretending that he begins to "drift in a world of his own"; a world of his own imagination that is full of lies that becomes his reality. In His world he is "laughing and gay like a clown" meaning that he has put on a mask that displays to others that he is fine; that his life is happy and filled with joyous moments although that could not be farther from the truth.

He is The Great Pretender "wearing his heart like a crown". A crown is a traditional headdress worn on the head of a king or queen symbolizing their power, authority, legitimacy, victory, triumph, honor, and glory. A crown is displayed on the head for all to take notice that the one wearing it is the ruler (in control) over his or her realms. The singer of this song pretends that he is in control of his hearts emotions by wearing it as crown so all can see that he has power over how he feels although he is heartbroken, in distress, and is really unable to move forward.

He says, "I play the game"; the game of hiding the truth of who he really is and pretends to be whom he thinks others want him to be and/or who he thinks he should be for other people. All the while he is hurting on the inside just going through the motions. "In life, the hypocrite is a person who masks [their] real self while playing a part for the audience. Taken over into the New Testament, it referred to one who assumes the mannerisms, speech, and character of someone else, thus hiding [their] true identity; the person is judging another from the back of the mask of [their] self-righteousness. Christianity requires that believers should be open and above-board. Their lives should be like an open book, easily read."[10]

Praying in public just like praying in private should be genuine, true to you and your situation, and always from a pure heart. At all times our prayers should be God-focused, not a time of trying to win the acceptance, approval, or acknowledgement of others. Praying in public is not a time to prove to people that you are devout and righteous in the things of God. Prayer done in private or public are both for the sole purpose of communicating with God, not others. Prayer is not a time to put on a performance for others, but a time of Holy Concealment.

---

10 Overstreet, Peggy. "Greek Word Studies." Greek Word Studies Blogspot. April 2, 2007. http://greekwordstudies.blogspot.com/2007/04/hypocrisy.html.

Your prayer closet is a place of sacred and holy concealment.

4

Holy Concealment

To avoid the problem of wrong motives when they pray, Jesus tells His disciples to go into their closets. *"But thou, when thou prayest, enter into thy closet, and when thou hast shut thy door, pray to thy Father which is in secret; and thy Father which seeth in secret shall reward thee openly" (v6).*

Closets as we all know are spaces that are designated to be used for the sole purpose of storage or privacy. When Jesus instructs his disciples to pray in their closet He is not necessarily concerned about the place where they pray, but He is more concerned about them drawing attention to their self-righteousness as they pray. In this instance Jesus is directing His disciples to a place of privacy (intimacy).

The Greek word used here for "closet" is *tameion* which means "an inner storage chamber or a secret room."[1] A prayer closet is a secret room; a private appointed space where you can met with God alone. It is "a place of sacred and holy concealment"[2]. Your secret space can be a literal closet, a designated room, a chair in the corner of your room, in your bathroom, outside on your porch with a cup of coffee etc. A "prayer closet" can be anywhere you experience uninterrupted time with God. Your prayer closet can sometimes be a space in your heart; a space that you don't allow others to come or give away to others, but it is only reserved for God. It's where you learn to enjoy the presence of God and experience his joy (Ps. 16:11).

The prayer closet is also a place where you go to find release, rest, and receive from God. When we go to God in prayer we are welcomed by Him to release all the burdens of life that are too much for us to cope with. To release in prayer is to gain relief from life's burdens. When we release to God in prayer we give our burdens over to God. We tell God what's going on, how we feel about what's going on, and how we need help to cope with what's going on. We release to Him to no longer have ownership or bear the responsibility of the outcome of what we are burdened with. They

1   "G5009 - tameion - Strong's Greek Lexicon (KJV)." Blue Letter Bible. Accessed 23 February, 2019. https://www.blueletterbible.org//lang/lexicon/lexicon.cfm?Strongs=G5009&t=KJV

2   John J. Parsons, "The Secret Place of the Most High: Dwelling in the Shadow of Shaddi," Hebrew for Christians, accessed February 20, 2019, https://www.hebrew4christians.com/Meditations/Secret/secret.html.

no longer belong to us to worry about, they are now His to deal with. To release is not just about giving our burdens to God but also about trusting God with what we have given to Him. It's about trusting what He does or doesn't do with what we have released to Him. When we release in prayer to God we find that we now have the space and ability to rest without worry in our hearts and thoughts, as well as being physically and spiritually relieved. Rest is the source of fulfillment, enjoyment, and contentment in our lives.

There is a tradeoff that happens when we come to God in prayer. As we release to Him we gain rest and because we are rested we are now able to receive from the Spirit of God who gives us what thoughts, understanding, wisdom, and knowledge that is needed to function in this life. When we are weary, burdened down, and overwhelmed with life, it is hard to hear the voice of God. These are the times when we say things like "I can't hear God" or "God isn't saying anything". When life is happening we want to know: Is this God? Is this what God is telling me to do? Is God trying to get my attention in this situation? We feel confused and deficient when it comes to hearing Gods voice. But because we have not come to God in the secret place and closed the door to release, rest, and receive from Him we are unable to hear His voice. Spending time alone in prayer with God is where we learn "how to listen to the voices of promise and seduction and decide how to adjudicate them, to hear better the true voice of assurance and to notice quickly the seductive voice of unfaith."[3] Spending time alone in prayer with God helps us to focus on His voice alone.

When we make time to escape from a world of busyness to a world of serenity through solitude, we are able to allow the frustration and anxiety of life to fade away. Psalm 91 speaks of the blessings associated with being in the secret place. It says that those who live in the secret place *"shall abide under the shadow of the Almighty"*. They will say of the Lord, *"He is my refuge and my fortress: my God; in him will I trust"*. God is our secret place and our habitation. The secret place is a place of protection, a place that's not susceptible to outside influence, and a place of sole reliance on God. The beauty in having a "closet" is that it frees us from disturbance, distraction, and deceptive eavesdroppers that keeps us from having the kind of prayer life that allows us to be vulnerable before God.

Jesus didn't just advise His disciples to spend time alone with God in prayer, but He himself took His own advice. Withdrawing to a solitary place to pray, he knelt down and prayed (Luke 22:39-46). *"Very early in the morning, while it was still dark, Jesus got up, left the house*

---

3   Walter Brueggemann and Richard A. Floyd, *A Way Other Than Our Own: Devotions for Lent* (Louisville, Kentucky: Westminster John Knox Press, 2017), 8.

and went off to a solitary place, where he prayed" (Mark 1:35). Jesus teaches us that it is good and necessary to spend time alone with God in prayer no matter who we are. If the Son of God himself felt it necessary to spend time alone with God then we should too. Dallas Willard in his book Hearing God, says that "people are meant to live in an ongoing conversation with God, speaking and being spoken to."[4] Hearing the voice of God is a must in order to journey successfully through this life. In today's society where many of us are immensely attached to social media, having a prayer closet is what we need to help quiet our hearts and settle our spirits, in order to hear Gods voice.

In Isaiah chapter 30, the people of Israel are about to be attacked by the Assyrian army. The Assyrians were powerful and prepared to attack at any moment. Israel is trying to figure out what they should do to get out of what their disobedience got them into in the first place. They are worried and overwhelmed because they are faced with a problem that is out of their control and like many of us instead of turning to God, they sought the advice of those they thought had the ability, the power, and influence to do for them, what only God could do.

4   Dallas Willard, Hearing God: Developing a Conversational Relationship with God, updated and expanded / lbby j ed. (Downers Grove, Ill.: IVP Books, 2012), 21.

"The Lord said, look at these children. They don't obey me. They make plans, but they don't ask me to help them. They make agreements with other natins, but my Spirit does not want those agreements. These people are adding more and more sins to the ones they have already done. They are going down to Egypt for help, but they did not ask me if that was the right thing to do. They hope they will be saved by the Pharaoh. They want Egypt to protect them. But I tell you, hiding in Egypt will not help you.

Pharaoh will not be able to protect you. Your leaders have gone to Zoan, and your representatives have gone to Hanes. But they will be disappointed. They are depending on a nation that cannot help them. Egypt is useless — it will not help. Egypt will bring nothing but shame and embarrassment", *(Is 30:1-5 ERV)*.

The people of Israel refused to listen to the instructions of God from the prophets and they insisted on doing things their way. The only thing God asked of them was to repent and seek His presence in solitude in order to be delivered from defeat at the hands of the Assyrians. God tells them that *"In returning and rest shall ye be saved; in quietness and in confidence shall be your strength: and ye would not"*, *(Is 30:15)*. Instead of spending time alone with God in solitude, like the children of Israel, many people would much rather seek the support and wisdom of others. All God wanted the people of Israel to do was to come to Him in silence (solitude). He wanted them to spend time in His presence. Many of us suffer the silence of God because we refuse to come to Him and spend time in His presence in quietness (solitude).

Throughout history, solitary confinement has been used as a form of torture and punishment. Solitary confinement is distinguished by living in single cells with little or no meaningful contact with other inmates. The prison system is designed to be a system of separation, separating law abiding citizens from those who break the law as a form of rehabilitation. In the 19th century when the prison system was first presented, the idea was that prisoners would find remorse for their unlawful acts through silent reflection of their behavior. Instead, their time of silent reflection was viewed by them as a form of punishment that was unpleasant and a waste of time because it was not something they choose to do willfully, it was given to them as a consequence of their actions. What the prison system did not understand was that solitude is not something we do by being force into it unwillingly, however, it must be willfully and purposely entered into in order to experience the effects of remorse and rehabilitation. In addition, solitude must not only be entered into willingly and purposely but it must be done in the presence of God. Without the presence of God in your time of solitude there is no release, rest, receiving, or even restoring going on. It's just a time of boredom that brings about more defeat, anger, sadness, etc. Solitude should not be seen as a form of punishment, but as the joy of willfully and purposefully being alone with God. Willful and purposeful solitude is beneficial because it's what takes us from the state of our mindlessness routine of everyday life into a higher conscious state of mind which reconnects us with God and His purposes for our life.

I've always admired St. Francis of Assisi for his discipline in the practice of solitude. St. Francis was an Italian Catholic friar, deacon, and preacher. He lived a life devoted to Christianity. He was often known to go away quietly to commune with God in solitude, in the caves surrounding Assisi, Province of Perugia, Italy. There he would spend time in worship and prayer. On several occasion his companions would find St. Francis totally engulfed in the presence of God. It was his time spent alone with God that fueled him with the strength needed to sustain him for long days of ministry.

While many of us can identify with having busy lives filled with long days like St. Francis, the secret to him being able to handle those long days was because of his time spent alone with God in solitude. This is something we need to learn from St. Francis. Instead of being driven by the need to be busy doing things, mattering not if it is a good thing, but focusing on rather or not it is a God thing. This means that we need to learn to be intentional, willing, and purposeful about cultivating a discipline of spending time alone with God in solitude and prayer, allowing God to speak to us. "God's speaking to us is intended to develop into an intelligent, freely cooperative relationship between mature people who love each other with the richness of genuine love."[5] In solitude our relationship is developed with God and the more time we spend with Him in solitude listening for His voice, the more we'll be able to recognize His voice; *To him the porter openeth; and the sheep hear his voice: and he calleth his own sheep by name, and leadeth them out. And when he putteth forth his own sheep, he goeth before them, and the sheep follow him: for they know his voice. And a stranger will they not follow, but will flee from him: for they know not the voice of strangers, John 10:3-5.*

---

5   Dallas Willard, Hearing God: Developing a Conversational Relationship with God, updated and expanded / lbby j ed. (Downers Grove, Ill.: IVP Books, 2012), 21.

Repeating things fills up time, but it does not prove our devotion or better our chances of God hearing us.

5

Stop Repeating That

"Can you hear me now?" is a slogan used by Cello Partnership, who operated under the name of Verizon Wireless in 2002. The slogan was one of the company's marketing strategies to help boost sales and maintain their number one status in the cellular phone industry. During this time, the much smaller cellular phone competitors such Cingular Wireless and Sprint PCS began what they called price wars where they offered lower priced calling plans.

Verizon took a hit and experienced a slight decline in their clientele because of the price wars, however they were determined not to get involved in that type of marketing. What Verizon did was enlisted the help of Bozell, a New York based advertising agency who came up with the famous slogan "Can you hear me now?"

The slogan "Can you hear me now?" was the way Verizon mocked its competitors. They did this after learning through research, that their service was the most dependable in the industry at the time. During the price wars Cingular Wireless did exceptionally well to inquire new customers, however they were likely to experience four times more dropped calls or lost of service than Verizon. Knowing this, rather than dropping prices to compete in the price wars Verizon focused on what made them a better provider than all the rest. Verizon understood that they had the capability to sustain their customer's phone calls without them having to experience dropped calls or lost signals in the middle of conversations. Never would they have to ask the person on the other end of the call "Can you hear now?" because they were with the best in the business.

Many of Cingular Wireless customers were attracted by the low priced services provided but never anticipated having to deal with the frustration of not being able to hear their callers. Though they initially saved money going with a lower priced service plan, they ultimately paid the cost of not having service and were unable to communicate with their callers on the other end of the receiver. Important messages were unable to be heard because of dropped calls or lost signals; some people missed important business deals, some missed job opportunities, then again some missed dinner plans, while others might have missed an emergency call. Whatever the message may have been, they were unable to hear it and they were left repeating the phrase "Can you hear me now?" "Can you hear me now?" "Can you hear me now?"

Many of us were victims of having to use this phrase "Can you hear me now?" because we chose to go the cheaper route and use a service provider that was faulty and unreliable. The funny thing about this slogan, "Can you hear me now?" used by Verizon is that we would repeat it over and over again as if doing so would connect us to the caller on the other line. The service connection was faulty and nothing we could say or do would fix the connection. If the connection wasn't working then nothing we were saying was going to get through no matter how many times we repeated it. The same is true in our prayer lives. Repeating words or phrases in prayer doesn't connect us to God or gain His attention. If our relationship with God is not hard-wired with humble submission to the will of God, then we pray in vain. Jesus warns the disciples about using vain repetitions in Matthew 6:7, *"but when ye pray, use not vain repetitions, as the heathen do: for they think that they shall be heard for their much speaking. Be not ye therefore like unto them: for your Father knoweth what things ye have need of, before ye ask him."* Jesus isn't saying that we can't be persistent in our prayers by continuously praying the same request. Being persistent in prayer is not the same as using vain repetitions. After all, Jesus taught us that we should "Always pray and not give up" (Luke 18:1). He himself was found in the Garden of Gethsemane repeating His prayer, *"Father let this cup pass me"* (Matthew 26:39, 42, 44) three times.

The parable of the unjust judge who lacks compassion is repeatedly approached by a poor widow who is seeking justice (Luke 18:1-8). Originally the judge rejects her request several times but eventually he honors her request so he will not be worn out by her persistence. This parable that Jesus shares with his disciples teaches the importance of being persistence in praying their request continuously and never giving up. What Jesus was doing in Chapter 6 of Matthew "was condemning the shallow repetition of words by those who did not have a personal relationship with the Father."[1] Jesus' warning against vain repetitions means we should avoid vain or meaningless words and repetition in our prayers. Repeating things fills up time, but it does not prove our devotion or better our chances of God hearing us. The pagans focused on how they delivered their prayers, repeating the right words in the right order. They often repeated the names of their

---

1   Bruce B. Barton, *Matthew*, Life Application Bible Commentary (Wheaton, Ill.: Tyndale House Publishers, 1996), 113.

gods as a way to get a blessing. These types of people are like the duck on the Aflac commercial that walks around quacking "Aflac, Aflac, Aflac", (the company's name) to prospective customers, in an effort to get them to purchase their insurance policy. For me after about 3 quacks I get annoyed, and many of you too. I'm sure God gets annoyed when all we do is repeat over and over again meaningless words in prayer in an attempt to get Him to answer our request. Prayer is not heaping up meaningless words, but it's engaging in sincere communication with our heavenly Father, with a heart that is humbly submitted to His will.

I remember as a little girl my father would give me anything I wanted. However, the key to getting what I wanted from him was that I had to ask him first. It wasn't that he didn't know what I needed or wanted. You see, whenever I needed or wanted something I would always go to my mom, and tell her to ask my dad for me. Her response to me would be "You need to go to him yourself and ask for what you want." But, before I would even make it to my dad to ask for what I wanted, my mom would have already informed him. Jesus tells His disciples that there is no need to pray like the heathens, informing their gods of what they needed, because the disciples' God, whom they have relationship with, already knows what they need before they ask. We as believers don't pray from a position of informing God as if He has no clue of what is happing in our lives. When we pray, we are inviting God into our lives. We invite Him to fellowship with us, we invite Him to develop us, and we invite Him to reveal our dependency on Him. But we don't invite Him to inform Him. When we understand that God is already aware of our concerns there is no need to repeat them over and over again to Him, but we must simply invite Him into our concerns.

Pray like this.

6

And it Goes Like This

After Jesus tells His disciples "who not to be like" when they pray, He then instructs them on things they are to implement in their prayer while in the closet. It's Jesus' desire that the disciples pray effectively in order to be heard by God and to receive answers to their prayers. It appears that many people are praying these days with all the prayer lines, prayer services, and corporate prayer meetings going on, but yet, many people still have not seen answers to prayer.

I am reminded of the comedian Eddie Murphy in the 1986 movie drama entitled The Golden Child. Eddie Murphy plays a detective by the name of Chandler Jarrell, who has a specialty of finding missing children. "After the disappearance of The Golden Child—a young monk boy with special magical abilities who was kidnapped by an an evil sorcerer,"[1] Chandler is told that he is the "Chosen One", the one who was sought out to find and protect the "Golden Child."

Chandler thinks that it's a joke at first, "but as the investigation advances he learns that supernatural forces are real and only he can put a stop to the wicked Sardo Numspa (Charles Dance) and his minions."[2] He is told that there is a sacred knife (dagger) that he needed that would help him in protecting The Golden Child. In order to obtain the scared knife he had to request it from the High Priest of the temple where the knife was being kept. He couldn't just ask for the knife in any manner, nor could the woman who was assisting him ask for the knife on his behalf. He had to ask for it himself, and do so in a strategic way in order for the High Priest to provide him with the knife's location.

While standing before the High Priest in the temple, the High Priest "merely ask[ed] him to say, 'I want the knife' which he does, saying just that. However, the fact that he is somewhat desecrating centuries-old customs and religious rituals by asking in such a semi-mocking tone as he spins a type of prayer wheel that is attached to a portion of the entrance pillar asking

---

1   Unknown, "Movie Review: The Golden Child," The Attack of The Couch Potato, May 22, 2015, https://attackofthecouchpotato.wordpress.com/tag/the-golden-child/.

2   Ibid.

for the knife, (which he does just [as] a hip-hop DJ would a vinyl record), turn[ing] a simple request into"[3] mockery that offends the High Priest and all the Priest present in the temple. His first request was denied, not because he didn't ask but because of the way he asked. It was not in line with how he was required to ask the High Priest. He quickly realizes that his first request wasn't appropriate and he asks again spinning the prayer-wheel using a more reverential approach of respect for the High Priest, and the temple culture. When he did, his request for the knife from the High Priest was answered.

Similar to the disciples, it wasn't that they were not praying. They understood the scriptures and the importance of praying daily; it was on this that they emphasized and prided themselves. The problem was that they were not praying in a manner that would lead to answered prayer. Therefore, Jesus gives the disciples the things necessary to implement in their prayers, to ensure they received answers to their prayers. Jesus teaches the disciples The Lord's Prayer. He gives them The Lord's Prayer as an index for prayer. Index prayers were a collection of brief sentences, each of which suggested what should be prayed for.

---

3   Vince Leo, "The Golden Child," Qwipster Movie Reviews, accessed May 21, 2019, http://www.qwipster.net/goldenchild.htm.

The Lord's Prayer illustrates the type of prayer that provides a pattern for properly ordering the priorities of the kingdom; first God, then human needs. The Lord's Prayer is a set of index sentences covering every element of prayer; it states for us in topical form the ingredients necessary for effective prayer. Whether you are in worship, intercession, petition, or thanksgiving, the Lord's Prayer covers it all.

Jesus tells his disciples:

- Go in your closet, shut the door and when you pray *address* God for who He is. *"After this manner therefore pray ye: our father which art in heaven, hallowed be thy name."* When we address someone we are making certain that the person we are talking to knows that we are talking to them and only them. In addition when we address someone in conversation we call them by name, a name which identifies who they are. Addressing God as Father identifies who He is and who He is in our relationship with Him; Him as Father and us as His children. It also shows our humble submission to His authority and that we regard Him as holy.

- Go in your closet, shut the door and when you pray *acknowledge* God's kingdom rule. *"Thy kingdom come."* In a blog entitled, 4 Ways to Acknowledge Others, Linda A. Curtis writes that "Acknowledgement is one element of relational dialogue that is most often overlooked."[4] Many times we find ourselves praying for blessings from God without acknowledging Him first. When we acknowledge we are letting someone know that we are aware of something and that we agree with what we are aware of and are accepting. God's kingdom rule "refers to god's spiritual reign."[5] As we acknowledge God's kingdom it is to pray the hastening of his kingdom here in the earth and that more people will receive Christ in their hearts and be a part of God's kingdom.

- Go in your closet, shut the door and when you pray *accept* God's sovereign will. *"Thy will be done in earth, as it is in heaven."* This phrase shows our submission to the will of God. The will of God is that we would accept what He allows to happen in our lives. There are many times that when we go in prayer that God will respond in ways that we may or may not agree with. Maybe we felt like there could have been a better plan or outcome. God does all things according to His will and it's in the closet where

---

4 Linda Curtis, "4 Ways to Acknowledge Others," Linda Curtis, November 11, 2015, https://lindaacurtis.com/4-ways-to-acknowledge-others/.

5 Bruce B. Barton, Matthew (Wheaton, Ill.: Tyndale House Publishers, 1996), 114.

we come to grips with God's will. God's will is His Holy purposes that has been ordained to take place in our life.

- Go in your closet, shut the door and when you pray *ask* God for what you need. *"Give us this day, our daily bread."* This request is one of asking for His provision on a daily basis. Our daily bread speaks of everything necessary to sustain us in life; the money and food we need on a daily basis. This petition implies dependence on God for the supply of daily needs. In prayer we are to come to God in a spirit of humble dependence, asking Him to provide what we need and to sustain us from day to day. We have been invited to go to Him and ask for our daily bread and He will not fail to provide for us.

- Go in your closet, shut the door and when you pray seek God for *amnesty*. *"And forgive us our debts as we also have forgiven our debtors."* To obtain amnesty is to be granted a pardon of our offenses. This is a request to receive forgiveness of sins that we confess to Him that we have done. To forgive completely requires one of the most difficult of all amendments, but just as we need forgiveness, so do others. We must be honest about our faults, and unless we have a forgiving attitude it is impossible to receive divine forgiveness from God (Mat 6:14, 15; 18:21-35).

- Go in your closet, shut the door and when you pray request God to *administrate* your steps. *"And do not lead us into temptation, but deliver us from evil."* To administrate is to manage or control the function of an operation. When we ask God to administrate in prayer it is a cry to God out of a weak flesh, out of grief of falling short of God's standard of holiness. We are to pray, not that we may be spared the trial but that when it comes we will remain faithful to Christ and will not succumb to temptation or the evil one.

- Go in your closet, shut the door and when you pray, again *acknowledge* His rule and accept His will. *"For thine is the kingdom, and the power, and the glory, forever."* (See above acknowledge)

As previously stated in this chapter, Jesus used index prayers as prayer suggestions for the disciples, it was not a set way of praying that Jesus himself prayed or asked his disciples to pray, but it illustrates the type of prayer that provides a pattern for properly ordering the priorities of the kingdom, first God, then human needs. These index prayers are applicable to believers today. This is the way in which Jesus was teaching His disciples to pray and this is the way you and I should pray, "When we pray".

While it is important to gain knowledge through studying, reading, memorizing scripture, praying and mediating it should not be the focus. As we enter into our prayer closet, we are to seek the Lord and allow Him to speak to our hearts. As this becomes our prayer pattern our relationship with God will become more personal and more powerful.

What happens in the closet stays in the closet.

7

Close the Door

In this day and age where the majority of society is so accepting of many different types of lifestyles that do not equate to a lifestyle of holiness, numerous people have found it safe to do what is called "come out of the closet", though it has long time been what the church would consider as an evil act to do so. "Coming out of the closet" is loosely understood to be when someone is willing to talk in public about things that are to be kept unspoken of. In essence, it's taking private matters and making them public.

The city of Las Vegas has a well known slogan that says, "What happens in Vegas, stays in Vegas". Meaning "it happened. It only happened there. And it happened far enough away to not have any negative effect on 'the here and now'. Anyone who wasn't there at the time need not know about it."[1] But because you were there you get to keep the memories of what happened there. "What happens in the closet stays in the closet". This meaning is what Jesus alludes to when He tells the disciples to go into their closet; a private place to pray and close the door. Closed doors create effective barriers between what is inside the room and what is outside the room.

Many of us grew up being educated on fire safety habits in school and even on our jobs. Over the course of our lives we've learned fire drills, escape routes, designated meeting places, the importance of having smoke detectors, and the stop, drop, and roll method. However, I can't say that I recall talking about closing the door as much as fire drills. The Underwriters Laboratories Firefighter Safety Research Institute (ULFSBI) has proven through their research that closing doors is more vital than ever before. ULFSBI is an organization that is devoted to "providing independent research, knowledge and training for the fire safety community and for the protection of people and property around the world."[2] They have an initiative called Close Your Door. " The

---

1   Mister B, "What Happens in Vegas Stays in Vegas," Urban Dictionary, November 18, 2006, https://www.urbandictionary. com/definephp?term= what%20happens%20in%20Vegas%20stays%20in%20Vegas.

2   The UL Firefighter Safety Research Institute, "Spread the Word," Close Your Door, accessed May 5, 2019, https://closeyourdoor.org/#facts.

Close Your Door safety initiative comes as the result of over 10 years of research... after proving that a closed door could potentially save lives in a fire, [and they have] committed to share [their] finding[s] with the world."[3] Their mission is to educate the public on how closing their bedroom doors before going to sleep "can save lives by slowing the spread of fire and smoke."[4] If your bedroom door is left open while you are sleep and a fire starts, the fire will have the ability to spread at an increased rapid speed because oxygen from the room fuels fires. However, when your door is closed you reduce the speed of the fire and its toxins. When we close our doors in prayer it eliminates the spread of your personal issues to those who are toxic and fueled with negativity and gossip. Closing your door in prayer is more vital than you know.

In chapter 44 of Ezekiel, The Spirit of the Lord took Ezekiel up in a vision while he was in captivity along with the people of Israel because of their disobedience and stubbornness toward the Lord's commands. In that vision the Spirit of the Lord brought him into the inner court to show him the East Gate of the sanctuary that would be rebuilt in the future. Then the Lord said to him, *"This gate shall be shut, it shall not be opened, and no man shall*

---

3   The UL Firefighter Safety Research Institute, "Spread the Word," Close Your Door, accessed May 5, 2019, https://closeyourdoor.org/#facts.

4   Ibid.

enter in by it; because the Lord, the God of Israel, hath entered in by it, therefore it shall be shut. It is for the prince; the prince, he shall sit in it to eat bread before the Lord; he shall enter by the way of the porch of that gate, and shall go out by the way of the same", *(Ezekiel 44:1-3)*. Ezekiel is instructed that The East Gate must remain shut because the presence of the Lord had entered in through the gate. The East Gate represents the door of the sanctuary that is to remain shut, and the sanctuary represents the closet or sacred space where the Lord entered. He also shares with Ezekiel that the only person who can enter the gate is the prince. The gate is closed shut to everyone and not open or available to anyone else but the prince. The prince represents the one who is in charge of protecting the presence of The Lord.

God's presence "dwell[ed] in the temple built by Solomon after his fervent and humble prayer (2 Chronicles 6-7). God chose to allow His presence—again evident through the radiance and splendor of His glory—to remain in the temple for centuries. Yet after the Jews had proven their determination to continue in false idolatrous worship, the presence of God did eventually leave the Jerusalem temple, (Ezekiel 8-10)."[5] God is showing Ezekiel that when his

---

5 United Church of God, "The Departure of God's Glory: Ezekiel 10," United Church of God Bible Commentary, August 28, 2018, http://bible.ucg.org/bible-commentary/Ezekiel/Glory-of-God-departs-from-the-temple-with-the-cherubim/.

presence is back in the temple it must be protected behind closed doors from false idolatrous worship. In our sacred spaces we must be protective of the presence of God by closing the door and shutting people out that don't have a reverence for the presence of God. This is not just a nice room to pray but a Holy place that must be respected and protected otherwise God's presence won't show up. If His presence doesn't show up in our prayer then we are just having a talk with ourselves to no avail. Not only does closed doors in prayer create effective barriers between what is inside a room and what is outside a room, but it also establishes a sacred space, forging an atmosphere of vulnerability between you and God. In genuine prayer with God you will find yourself in a vulnerable position offering your total self over to Him, the good, the bad, and the ugly.

Closing your door in prayer is liken unto a husband and wife relationship. When they enter into their bedroom and shut the door (holy concealment) the children (those who are not privileged to be present to watch you press through your proclivities) are not to come in because intimacy (prayer) is taking place behind the closed door. In 1978 Teddy Pendergrass sang a hit song titled, "Close the Door". In the song he sings these lyrics to the woman whom he loves:

Close the door, Let me give you what you've been waiting for,
  Baby I got so much love to give, I want to give it all to you,

Close the door, No need to worry no more, Let's bring this day to a pleasant end Girl it's me and you now, I've waited all day long just to hold you in my arms, And it's exactly like I thought it would be, Me loving you and you loving me, Close the door.[6]

The intimacy of your relationship with God is built behind closed doors where there is no restriction, no interruption, and no distraction from other people. Your closet is not only a secret place but it is also a safe space for you where you can feel confident that you will not be exposed to the discrimination, criticism, or physical harm of others. What happens in the closet stays in the closet! Why? Because some of the things you struggle with in life, many people aren't mature enough to be privileged, to be present, to watch you press, through your proclivities. Some things you can't tell your prayer partner, you can't tell your spouse, and you can't tell your best friend. They would not understand. Therefore you must close the door.

Elisha understood this concept very well when he prayed for the Shunammite's dead son. *"He went in therefore, and shut the door upon them twain, and prayed unto the LORD", (2 Kings 4:33).* He understood the importance of what needed to be done and He did not need any distractions from onlookers or any publicity for himself. His sole concern was the resurrecting power of God for

---

6   Kenny Gamble and Leon Huff, *Close the Door* (Philadelphia, Pennsylvania: Philadelphia International Records, 1978).

the young boy. He was focused on engaging God so intently that nothing or no one around mattered. His closing the door "denoted his desire for privacy. The prophet practiced what he preached to others. In the miracle recorded at the beginning of chapter four, Elisha had bidden the widow "shut the door upon" herself and her sons (2 King 4:4) so as to avoid ostentation, and here Elisha follows the same course. He was about to engage the Lord in a most urgent and special prayer, and that is certainly something which calls for aloneness with God."[7]

What happens in the closet stays in the closet! And if you weren't in the closet with me then you have no clue what happened. Only I have the memory of this life changing, spiritual transforming experience, and for this I am granted a public reward in exchange for my private request. When God rewards you people will ask "How did you get what you got?" Just tell them, "It happened in the closet!" How did you forgive them? "It happened in the closet!" How did you learn to love them? "It happened in the closet!" How did your marriage get restored? "It happened in the closet!" How did you get that job? "It happened in the closet!" How did you get healed? "It happened in the closet!" How did your family come back together? "It happened in the closet!" How did you learn to trust God like you do? "It happened in the closet!

---

7   Arthur Walkington Pink, Gleanings from Elisha: His Life and Miracles (Chicago: Moody Press, 1972), 94.

How to Create a Sacred Space

1. Designate a space, room, or closet in your home or office. You may want to furnish it with a chair, table, a lamp, a notebook, a bible, a prayer shawl, a pillow, etc....

2. Schedule a time. It may help if you set a regular time for when you will spend time with God. As you become more consistent in spending time with God in prayer you will not only have a regular scheduled time but you will begin to sense when God is calling you to a time of prayer alone with Him outside of your regular scheduled time.

3. Get in there. Be intentional about utilizing the space.

4. Sit still and quiet. Center yourself by quoting a scripture, a word, or phrase to still your thoughts.

5. Keep the Space Sacred. The only thing done in that space should be prayer.

Appendix 1

The Lord's Prayer Scripture Comparison Outline

Outine	Matthew 6:9-13 (KJV)	Luke 11:2-4 (KJV)
		And he said unto them
	After this manner therefore pray ye:	*When ye pray, say*
Worship	Our Father which art in heaven, Hallowed be thy name.	Our Father which art in heaven, Hallowed be thy name.
Submission to His Sovereign Rule	Thy kingdom come.	Thy kingdom come.
Submission to His Sovereign Will	Thy will be *done in earth, as it is in heaven.*	Thy will be done, *as in heaven, so in earth.*
Petition and Intercession	*Give us this day our daily bread.*	*Give us day by day our daily bread.*
Confession and Forgiveness	*And forgive us our debts, as we forgive our debtors.*	*And forgive us our sins; for we also forgive every one that is indebted to us.*
Watchfulness and Deliverance	And lead us not into temptation, but deliver us from evil.	And lead us not into temptation, but deliver us from evil.
Worship	For thine is the kingdom, and the power, and the glory, for ever. Amen.	

Appendix 2

The Lord's Way to Pray Bible Study

The Lord's Prayer is not a set way of praying that Jesus himself prayed or asked his disciples to pray, but it illustrates the type of prayer that provides a pattern for properly ordering the priorities of the kingdom, first God, then human needs. The Lord's Prayer wasn't and still isn't meant to be said by routine. Rather, Jesus was using the same manner of instruction that the Jews used. He was teaching the disciples an index for prayer. Index prayers were a collection of brief sentences, each of which suggested a subject for prayer. The Lord's Prayer is a set of index sentences covering every element of prayer. The Lord's Prayer states for us in topical form the ingredients necessary for effective prayer. The Lord's Prayer covers ever topic of prayer. Whether you are in worship, intercession, petition, or thanksgiving, The Lord's Prayer covers it all.

Effective prayer comes from relationship with the Father. In order to pray The Lord's way you must first get to know Him and His ways through His word. We have been praying, but only out of what we have learned to memorize. Some of us have not recognized that our prayer lives have been powerless and unable to effect or change our surroundings. It is because we are relying on what we learned as a babe in Christ. Don't simply recite The Lord's Prayer as a part of your daily routine, but use it as the guide it was meant to be. Personalize your prayers with sincerity of the heart, and watch God move on your behalf.

Review the Text: Matthew 6:9-13

V9 Pray then like this: Our Father who art in heaven, Hallowed be thy name.

<u>Worship of the Father</u>:

- When you come to God in prayer you are coming to one who is greater and mightier than yourself. Worship is the first essential to prayer.

- Acknowledge your intimate relationship with God (Romans 8:15 Abba/Father)

- Acknowledge your relationship with Jesus. Not until you receive Jesus Christ as your Lord and Savior do you become a child of God.

  - *John 14:6 Jesus saith unto him, I am the way, the truth, and the life: no man cometh unto the Father, but by me.*

  - *John 8:19 Then said they unto him, Where is thy Father? Jesus answered, Ye neither know me, nor my Father: if ye had known me, ye should have known my Father also.*

- To hallow God's name is to make or set apart as holy; to respect or honor greatly. His name is to be regarded as holy and reverenced above all others. To acknowledge His worth.

  - *Ps 8:9 "O LORD our Lord, how excellent is thy name in all the earth!"*

  - *Exodus 20:7 You should not take the Lords name in vain. God's people hallow His name by living according to His will. If they do not then they profane His name.*

  - *Jeremiah 34:8-16 Polluted my name; by violating their covenant made before God in his house; an act of shameless perjury.*

- The name of the Lord denotes not merely a title but includes all that by which He makes Himself known and all that He shows Himself to be. When you hallow God's name you testify to His character, you acknowledge and respect who He is and behave accordingly.

  - Elohim–Creator

  - El Elyon–The Most High (Sovereign-supreme authority)

  - Jehovah Tsidkenu–The Lord Our Righteousness

- Jehovah Jireh–The Lord Will Provide
- Jehovah Raah–The Lord My Shepherd
- Jehovah Shalom–The Lord Sends Peace
- Jehovah Nissi–The Lord My Banner
- Jehovah Rapha– The Lord That Healeth
- Jehovah Shammah–The Lord Is There

V10a Thy kingdom come.

<u>The Sovereign Rule of God</u>

- The kingdom of God is the sovereign rule of God manifested in Christ to defeat His enemies, creating a people over whom He reigns, and issuing in a realm or realms in which the power of His reign is experienced.

- We long for the coming of King Jesus; The kingdom of God is the redemptive rule of God in Christ defeating Satan and the powers of evil and delivering people "righteousness, peace, and joy in the Holy Spirit. Entrance into the kingdom means deliverance from the power of darkness accomplished by the new birth.

- Those who pray for the coming of the Kingdom know that they must intercede for lost souls. The kingdom cannot come until His body is complete, until the last sheep is brought into the fold, for He will not lose one of His.

- *Mt 24:14 And this good news of the kingdom will be given through all the world for a witness to all nations; and then the end will come.*

- *2 Peter 3:12-14 When you pray for the coming of His kingdom you are hastening the coming of the Lord. (John the Baptist preaching repent for the kingdom of God is at hand).*

V10b Thy will be done in earth, as it is in heaven.

<u>Submission to His Will</u>:

- The will of God is that men should obey his commandments, and be holy. To pray, then, that His will may be done in the earth as in heaven is to pray that his commandments, and His revealed will may be obeyed and loved. His commandments are perfectly obeyed in heaven, and his true children most passionately desire and pray that it may also be done on the earth. Mt 7:21, 26:42; John 4:34

- We are praying that God's perfect purpose is accomplished in the earth as in heaven. If you are praying for His kingdom to come then you are saying that you want His will to be done when He gets here.

V11 Give us this day, our daily bread.

Petition and Intercession:

- Asking for His provision. The word bread here denotes everything necessary to sustain life.

- This petition implies our dependence on God for the supply of our needs.

- God is our Sustainer and Provider. We must trust God daily to provide for what He knows we need. Exodus 16:16-25

V12 And forgive us our debts as we also have forgiven our debtors.

Confession and Forgiveness of Debts:

- We must be honest about our faults

- We must have a proper attitude in prayer so that God will hear from us. Unless we have a forgiving attitude we should not ask for nor will we receive divine forgiveness from God. Matthew 18:21-35

  - *James 5:16 Confess your faults one to another, and pray one for another, that ye may be healed. The effectual fervent prayer of a righteous man availeth much.*

  - *1 John 1:9 If we confess our sins, He is faithful and just to forgive us our sins, and to cleanse us from all unrighteousness.*

- *Matthew 6:14, 15 For if ye forgive men their trespasses, your heavenly Father will also forgive you: But if ye forgive not men their trespasses, neither will your Father forgive your trespasses.*

V13a And do not lead us into temptation, but deliver us from evil.

<u>Watchfulness and Deliverance</u>:

- It is a cry to God out of poverty of spirit, out of grief for falling short of His standard of Holiness. It is a cry that says spare me from needless trials and test in which I might find myself tempted.

  - *Jas 1:13-14 Let no man say when he is tempted, I am tempted of God: for God cannot be tempted with evil, neither tempteth he any man: But every man is tempted, when he is drawn away of his own lust, and enticed.*

- It is also a cry of awareness that acknowledges the reality of the evil one and of the Christian's warfare. It acknowledges that the flesh is weak.

  - *Mt 26:41 Watch and pray, that ye enter not into temptation: the spirit indeed is willing, but the flesh is weak.*

V13b For yours is the kingdom and the power and the glory forever, Amen.

<u>Worship: Thine is the Kingdom.</u>

- That is, thine is the reign or dominion. God has control over all these things.

  - *Psalms 24:1 The earth is the LORD'S, and the fullness thereof; the world, and they that dwell therein.*

<u>Thine is the Power:</u>

- God has power to accomplish what we ask. We are weak, and cannot do it; but God is almighty, and all things are possible with thee.

  - *Matthew 19:26 But Jesus beheld them, and said unto them, With men this is impossible; but with God all things are possible.*

<u>Thine is the Glory:</u>

- That is, thine is the honor and praise. Not our honor; but God's glory, God's goodness, will be displayed in providing for our wants; God's power, in defending us; God's praise, in causing thy kingdom to spread through the earth.

  - *Ps 19:1 The heavens declare the glory of God; and the firmament sheweth his handiwork.*

<u>Amen: "so let it be"</u>

- To support or confirm.

- Decree – an authoritative order, directive, or command enforced by Law. In our kingdom role, we must accept our God-given authority and effectively utilize our power through the spoken word.

Reading the Moment

⁵And when thou prayest, thou shalt not be as the hypocrites are: for they love to pray standing in the synagogues and in the corners of the streets, that they may be seen of men. Verily I say unto you, They have their reward. ⁶But thou, when thou prayest, enter into thy closet, and when thou hast shut thy door, pray to thy Father which is in secret; and thy Father which seeth in secret shall reward thee openly. ⁷But when ye pray, use not vain repetitions, as the heathen do: for they think that they shall be heard for their much speaking. ⁸Be not ye therefore like unto them: for your Father knoweth what things ye have need of, before ye ask him. ⁹After this manner therefore pray ye: Our Father which art in heaven, Hallowed be thy name. ¹⁰Thy kingdom come, Thy will be done in earth, as it is in heaven. ¹¹Give us this day our daily bread. ¹²And forgive us our debts, as we forgive our debtors. ¹³And lead us not into temptation, but deliver us from evil: For thine is the kingdom, and the power, and the glory, forever. Amen. **Matthew 6:5-13** *(KJV)*

1. How does Jesus say to pray?

2. What are three things that Jesus says to not to do in prayer?

3. In Daniel 6:10 Daniel made a point of leaving the windows open so that when he prayed he was able to be seen praying. Why does Jesus make the statement here that "when you pray go in your prayer closet and close the door" in an effort not to be seen while praying?

4. The Lord's Prayer states for us in topical form the ingredients necessary for effective prayer, list the topics that it covers.

5. Forgiveness is an essential part of salvation 1 John 1:9 says "If we confess our sins, he is faithful and just and will forgive us our sins and purify us from all unrighteousness." According to the text, what is required to have our sins forgiven?

6. Vain repetition does not mean that we cannot be persistent in prayer. In the Garden of Gethsemane, Jesus repeats His prayer three times, Matthew 26:39, 42, and 44. Why should we avoid vain repetition and pointless babble?

7. To whom are we praying to and what is our relationship with Him?

8. What are we asking when we pray that God's will may be done on earth as in heaven?

9. How does "give us this day our daily bread" reflect our dependence on God for daily provision?

10. What is implied by "for yours is the kingdom and the power and the glory forever, Amen?"

Reflecting the Moment:

1. What was the purpose of Jesus teaching on prayer?

2. How would you characterize those whom Jesus called hypocrites?

3. To hallow God's name is to make or set apart as holy; to respect or honor greatly. His name is to be regarded as holy and reverenced above all others. The name of the Lord denotes not merely a title but includes all that by which He makes Himself known and all that He shows Himself to be. What are some attribute of God that describes who he is?

4. How does praying in private benefit you?

Responding to the Moment:

1. What three things can you do to maintain an effective prayer life?

2. How does it make you feel knowing that God already knows what you need before you ask in prayer and it doesn't take many words?

Appendix 3

The Call to Prayer—Focused Scriptures

Prayer

1. Prayer is communication with God; it's us seeking wise counsel; considering a matter with God not friends and family, which is utterly important according to the numerous scriptures found in the bible that lets us know that prayer has no season (Luke 18:1, 21:36; 1 Thess 5:17; Eph 6:18; Rom 12:12).

2. Prayer is not an option or a choice. Prayer is your life line; you cannot survive without communication with God.

Ephesians 2:2; Luke 11:1,2a; Proverbs 18:21

The enemy has control of the air waves and in this endeavor we have to set out to take our authority over the airwaves (phone lines, emails, texting, television, radio, conversations, letters, books, newspapers, etc.)

Isaiah 50:4-5

It is important to arise in the morning before the start of you busy day to seek the Lord for instructions on how to handle daily life situations and circumstances.

The "tongue of the learned" is the tongue of those who themselves learned in the ways of God, and are able to teach others. God hath revealed unto us; or rather, hath given us a power and will to hear and receive his commands, when we awake to meet Him in prayer.

Luke 11:1-13

It is okay to ask the Lord for what you are in need of. The Father is ready and willing to give out good gifts. Gifts better than our earthly father would or have given us. With boldness (knowing we will receive) ask, seek, and knock and the thing you are asking will be given.

Points to pull out of this text that shows us keys to prayer:

1. Persistence is the key in prayer *(Genesis 18, 32:22-32; Luke 18:1-8).*

2. It doesn't matter the time; the hour; the day when you approach God in prayer

3. Be Bold; you have access to God *(Hebrew 4:14-16).*

Mark 11:12-26

Every believer should be, is to be, a house of prayer

There are four points to pull out of this text that affects our prayers:

1. Having the form of one who prays but have no prayer life (no prayer no power)

2. Be sure to fulfill your purpose that you will not be casted aside

3. Have faith in the prayers that you pray

4. The importance of forgiveness

Matthew 18:19, 20

You must understand the importance of agreeing with one another in prayer, how much more effective is prayer when we come on one accord with other believers. I encourage you to agree out loud as each person prays with a: yes Lord, amen, hallelujah, glory, etc. This not only shows agreement but also encourages the one who is praying at that time.

Points to pull out:

1. You must determine with others what you are agreeing on. Each person must have the same mind-set about the subject matter. Seeking, asking, and knocking for the same outcome.

2. Then you must ask and it will be done for you.

3. *In my name*, that is by Jesus authority.

4. The Spirit of God is in the midst, to quicken their prayers, guide their counsels, and answer their petitions.

James 5:13-19

This scripture passage lets you know that no matter what situation you are in, prayer is the answer. Many people hate to hear the response "just pray about it" when faced with a trying situation. However it is the best antidote to any problem.

Points to pull out:

1. Prayer is the answer (much prayer much power, no prayer no power).

2. Righteous is to be in right-standing with God.

3. The importance of being found righteous (the prayers of the righteous are powerful and effective).

4. Praying for one another.

Matthew 26:36-46

Could you not watch with me one hour? This is what Jesus asked His disciples that He took with Him to the Garden of Gethsemane. This passage teaches us one reason why I should pray.

Point to pull out of the texts:

1. Be not fooled, the betrayer will come and is coming. In your time of peace continue to find yourself in prayer, be alert, and aware. Be not deceive the betrayer has not ceased his attack

against the people of God. Do not sleep in your time of peace.

2. There is never a time that we should not find ourselves in constant prayer, no matter what situation we find ourselves in. We have got to learn to discipline and condition ourselves in prayer. *Colossians 4:2*

Bibliography

Anonymous, *God Is Good and God Is Great Prayer*

Arthur, Kay. *Lord, Teach Me to Pray in 28 Days*. Eugene, Or.: Harvest House Publishers, 1995.

B, Mister. "What Happens in Vegas Stays in Vegas." Urban Dictionary. November 18, 2006. https://www. urbandictionary.com/define.php?term=what%20 happens%20in%20Vegas%20stays%20in%20Vegas.

Barton, Bruce B. *Matthew*, Life Application Bible Commentary. Wheaton, Ill.: Tyndale House Publishers, 1996.

Barton, David. *New England Primer*, 7th ed. (Aledo, TX: WallBuilder Press, 1991).

Bloom, Dov. "What Us the Amidah? The Silent Prayer." Chabad. Accessed April 27, 2019. https://www.chabad.org/library/ article_cdo/aid/3834226/jewish/What-Is-the-Amidah-The-Silent-Prayer.htm.

Brueggemann, Walter, and Richard A. Floyd. *A Way Other Than Our Own: Devotions for Lent*. Louisville, Kentucky: Westminster John Knox Press, 2017.

Calhoun, Adele Ahlberg. *Spiritual Disciplines Handbook: Practices That Transform Us*, revised and expanded ed., Downers Grove, Illinois: IVP Books, an imprint of InterVarsity Press, 2015.

Curtis, Linda. "4 Ways to Acknowledge Others." Linda Curtis. November 11, 2015. https://lindaacurtis.com/4-ways-to-acknowledge-others/.

Foster, Richard J. *Streams of Living Water: Celebrating the Great Traditions of Christian Faith.* San Francisco: Harper San Francisco, 1998.

"G5009 - tameion - Strong's Greek Lexicon (KJV)." Blue Letter Bible. Accessed 23 February, 2019. https://www.blueletterbible. org//lang/lexicon/lexicon.cfm?Strongs=G5009&t=KJV

"G5273 - hypokritēs - Strong's Greek Lexicon (KJV)." Blue Letter Bible. Accessed 1 May, 2019. https://www.blueletterbible. org//lang/lexicon/lexicon.cfm?Strongs=G5273&t=KJV

Gamble, Kenny, and Leon Huff. *Close the Door.* Philadelphia, Pennsylvania: Philadelphia International Records, 1978.

Got Questions? Your Questions. Biblical Answers. "What Is the International House of Prayer (Ihop)?." February 14, 2019. https://www.gotquestions.org/International-House-of-Prayer-IHOP.html.

Gross, D Qwynn. *Teach Me to Pray: Learning to Pray Like Jesus.* Shippensburg, PA: Destiny Image Publishers, 2009.

Guiley, Rosemary Ellen. "The Importance of Prayer and Meditation." Unity: A Positive Path for Spiritual Living. Accessed May 21, 2019. http://www.unity.org/resources/articles/importance-prayer-and-meditation.

Hemphill, Kenneth S. *The Prayer of Jesus: Living the Lord's Prayer.* Nashville, TN: LifeWay Press, 2002.

Hodges, Chris. *Fresh Air: Trading Stale Spiritual Obligation for a Life-Altering, Energizing, Experience-it-everyday Relationship with God.* Carol Stream, IL: Tyndale House Publishers, 2012.

Hunt, T W., and Claude V. King. *Pray in Faith*. Growing Disciples Series. Nashville, Tenn.: LifeWay Press, 2007.

King, Claude. "Growing Disciples: Helping Christian Believers, Leaders, and Churches Obey the Final Command." Lifeway Christian Resources. June 25, 2014. http://blog.lifeway.com/ growingdisciples/8-steps-toward-becoming-a-house-of- prayer-for-the-nations/.

Lazio, Michael. "What Is a House of Prayer?" Bethel house of Prayer. Accessed April 27, 2019. https://bethelhouseofprayer.com/ about/what-is-a-house-of-prayer/.

Leo, Vince. "The Golden Child." Qwipster Movie Reviews. Accessed May 21, 2019. http://www.qwipster.net/goldenchild.htm.

"Matthew 6:5 (KJV) - And when thou prayest thou." Blue Letter Bible. Accessed 27 May, 2019. https://www.blueletterbible.org/kjv/ mat/6/5/s_935005

Oshman, Jennifer. "Six Reason the Church Needs Corporate Prayer." Unlocking The Bible. May 7, 2018. https://unlockingthebible. org/2018/05/six-reasons-the-church-needs-corporate-prayer/.

Overstreet, Peggy. "Greek Word Studies." Greek Word Studies Blogspot. April 2, 2007. http://greekwordstudies.blogspot. com/2007/04/hypocrisy.html.

Parsons, John J. "The Secret Place of the Most High: Dwelling in the Shadow of Shaddi." Hebrew for Christians. Accessed February 20, 2019. https://www.hebrew4christians.com/ Meditations/Secret/secret.html.

Pink, Arthur Walkington. Gleanings from Elisha: His Life and Miracles, Chicago: Moody Press, 1972.

Ram, Buck. *The Great Pretender*. Berkeley, CA: Peermusic Publishing, 1955.

Ritenbaugh, Richard T. "Topical Studies: Bible Verses About Hypocritical Prayers." Bible Tools. Accessed April 19, 2019. https://www.bibletools.org/index.cfm/fuseaction/Topical.show/RTD/cgg/ID/18091/Hypocritical-Prayers.htm.

Sproul, R.C. "The House of Prayer." Ligonier Ministries. Accessed May 21, 2019. http://www.ligonier.org/learn/devotionals/house-prayer/.

The Attack of The Couch Potato. "Movie Review: The Golden Child." May 22, 2015. https://attackofthecouchpotato.wordpress.com/tag/the-golden-child/.

The UL Firefighter Safety Research Institute, "Spread the Word," Close Your Door, accessed May 5, 2019, https://closeyourdoor.org/#facts.

Willard, Dallas. *Hearing God: Developing a Conversational Relationship with God*. updated and expanded / lbby j ed. Downers Grove, Ill.: IVP Books, 2012.

Zondervan. *Niv, Thinline Bible, Large Print, Bonded Leather, Black, Red Letter Edition*. Box ed.: Zondervan, 2011.

About the Author

Tammy has dedicated her life to serve God and His people. Driven by her passion to teach, mentor, and intercede for God's people in order to meet their needs. Tammy is known among her peers as a woman after God's own heart, and a woman purposed and destined to carry the gospel to those who are lost; as she increases daily in wisdom, and stature, and in favor with God and man.

With her down to earth personality she attracts young adults; allowing her to walk alongside them, helping to navigate them through life challenges with spiritual concepts. She also mentors single adults as they trust and lean on God in they're waiting season. Sharing with them her wisdom and knowledge gained through her own personal life experiences with the guidance of the Holy Spirit.

Tammy has an anointing for intercession that is undeniable. She is a sought after teacher/preacher of prayer, equipping intercessors and prayer teams everywhere she is called upon.

Tammy received her Bachelor of Arts in Organizational Speech Communications from Texas Southern University in December of 2011. She also received her Master of Divinity in May of 2014 from The Houston Graduate School of Theology. She then went on to study abroad at The Hebrew University of Jerusalem in Israel during the summer of 2014. There she studied Coexistence in the Middle East and experienced the challenges of human diversity overseas where civilizations, religions and cultures converge. Tammy is currently pursuing her Doctor of Ministry degree at The Houston Graduate School of Theology.

Tammy has a heart for missions, locally and globally. She has assisted in organizing clothing drives for the Trinity Mission School (Save-A-Child) in Kenya, Africa. She also partners with low-income apartment complex to feed families during the holidays and coordinate financial resources to be given out to different ministries that are in need of assistance. In the September of 2015 Tammy traveled to East Africa where she participated in missionary work at Maween House. Maween House is a nonprofit organization located in Kenya, East Africa. The mission of Maween House is to provide for the complete needs of orphaned and destitute children between the ages 3-7 years old.

Tammy currently resides in Houston, TX and works as a Hospice Chaplain providing spiritual and emotional support to those who have been given 6 months or less to live. Tammy volunteers at the Star of Hope Women's Shelter, participate in numerous outreach efforts in the community and is an advocate of breast cancer awareness and heart health awareness.

For more information or to book Tammy as a speaker, please visit www.tamsisaac.org or email: tammymisaac@aol.com.

She may also be reached via social media at:
FB: www.facebook.com/tammymisacc
IG:timandcompany